The Earl & the Fairy

Story & Art by Ayuko

Original Concept by Mizue Tani

From Cobalt Series *Hakushaku to Yosei Amai Wana Ni Wa Kiotsukete* (The Earl and the Fairy: Beware of Sweet Traps)

Last time in The Earl & the Fairy

Kidnapped?!

→Edgar practically kidnaps Lydia so she can help him find the Treasure Sword.

HAVE YOU ABDUCTED ME?!
NOW WHAT?!
ALL MY LUGGAGE IS ON THE OTHER SHIP!

Nineteenth-century England. Lydia Carlton can see fairies, but she is otherwise a completely normal girl. She is on her way to spend a holiday with her father in London when a young man named Edgar drags her into a struggle over the Treasure Sword of the legendary Blue Knight Earl. Claiming to be the earl's descendant, Edgar employs Lydia to help him find the sword, but he turns out to be a fraud. And to make matters worse, he may be a thief and murderer!

YOU ARE THE NEW BLUE KNIGHT EARL.
NEVER FORGET THAT THE MERROWS ...
...ARE NOW YOUR PEOPLE.

Receiving the Sword

←The Merrows have guarded the sword for centuries. Impressed by Lydia's quick thinking and Edgar's determination, they grant him the Treasure Sword.

Key Terms

The Earl and the Fairy Realm

The earl's official title is Lord Ibrazel. For generations, the one who holds that title has been a lord of the Fairy Realm. The people adore him as an honorable noble who appears in legends and folk tales.

In the name of Edward I...
...I declare that henceforth and for all time...
...the King of England shall welcome the Blue Knight into his court.

The Treasure Sword and the Star Sapphire

The Treasure Sword proves the earl's rank. The Star Sapphire in the hilt is also called the Merrow Star.

The First Blue Knight Earl

The founder of the Ashenbert family. He swore fealty to Edward I, who bestowed upon him his title and the Treasure Sword. According to legend, he led fairies in battle.

Edgar Ashenbert

He was born a noble but was sold into a harsh existence as a slave. With Lydia's help, he has become the Blue Knight Earl. He uses his talent for sweet talk to manipulate Lydia.

Lydia Carlton

A young woman who can see and converse with fairies. She is working hard to become a proper Fairy Doctor like her departed mother.

Nico

Lydia's sidekick fairy who looks like a cat. He puts on airs, fussing about his clothing and meals.

Raven

Edgar's faithful attendant. Possessed by a spirit of battle, his skills as a fighter are superb.

Commentary

[Fairy Doctor]

A specialist who can see and talk to fairies. Thoroughly versed in fairy lore, she can help resolve problems between fairies and humans.

The Earl & the Fairy

Clop
Clop
THE FOG HAS GROWN THICK, HASN'T IT?
HM ...?
OH... YES.
...

IT'S THE PERFECT DAY FOR SOMETHING **DREADFUL** TO HAPPEN.
A LADY LIKE YOU SHOULDN'T BE WAITING FOR A CARRIAGE ALONE.
YES... YOU'RE RIGHT.
I WAS SEPARATED FROM MY MAID.
I AM GRATEFUL FOR YOUR KINDNESS, MY LORD.
THINK NOTHING OF IT.
I AM LUCKY TO BE IN THE COMPANY ...
...OF ONE SO LOVELY.

N-NO... OF COURSE NOT.

EVERYONE SAYS YOU ARE A PERFECT GENTLEMAN.

TH-THUMP

...

IF ROSALIE KNEW ...

...SHE WOULD BE JEALOUS.

PARDON ME.

THE WIND BLEW A LEAF INTO YOUR HAIR.

KLATTER

KLATTER

THE LONDON FOG POSSESSES AN EVIL WILL.

DO YOU KNOW HOW MANY CHILDREN ...

...IT HAS SWALLOWED ...

...LADY DORIS?

KTAK
NO...
WE HAVE ARRIVED.
CHAK
BE CAREFUL, OR THE MALEVOLENT FOG ...
...WILL SWALLOW YOU.

EARL IBRAZEL...
LORD OF THE FAIRY REALM...
WHAT A MYSTERIOUS MAN.
DORIS!
!
ROSALIE ...
DIDN'T YOU GO ...
...TO HELP AT THE CHARITY BAZAAR?!
I SAW YOU IN THAT CARRIAGE!
WHAT WERE YOU DOING WITH EARL IBRAZEL?!
NO...
...YOU DON'T UNDER-STAND ...
WE JUST HAP-PENED TO MEET AND—
ARE YOU TRYING TO **LEAVE ME?**
OF COURSE NOT!

DORIS ...
...YOU'RE HIDING SOMETHING FROM ME!
I...
I'M NOT HIDING ANY-THING.
OH, REALLY?!
BUT WE PROMISED TO SHARE EVERY-THING!
WE SWORE TO THE FAIRY!!
THEN WHAT ...
...ARE THOSE SECRET LETTERS YOU'VE BEEN WRITING?

YOU ARE HIDING SOME-THING!
WELL, I'M THROUGH WITH YOU!
I NO LONGER CONSIDER YOU MY COUSIN!
I HOPE ...
...THE FOGMAN GETS YOU!
IF SOMETHING BAD HAPPENS, DON'T EXPECT ME TO HELP!

LET'S SWEAR TO THE FAIRY...
...THAT WE'LL NEVER KEEP SECRETS ...
...BECAUSE WE'RE BEST FRIENDS!

IF WE BREAK OUR VOW, MAY THE FOGMAN GET US!
THE FOGMAN ...
...IS A FAIRY KNOWN TO EVERY CHILD IN LONDON.
I'M TOO OLD TO BELIEVE IN FAIRY-TALES...
...BUT I'M STILL AFRAID OF HIM.

YOU SEE, I ONCE SAW A BOY...
...WHO HAD BEEN TAKEN BY THE FOGMAN.

I HOPE THE FOGMAN GETS YOU!

I WONDER WHAT WOULD HAPPEN ...
...IF HE REALLY DID TAKE ME.

MAYFAIR, WHERE LONDON'S FINEST MANSIONS ARE FOUND.

AN EARL PURCHASED THIS WHITE GRANDEUR...

...AFTER RETURNING TO ENGLAND FROM ABROAD.

AND FOR SOME REASON, I WORK HERE.

WH...

HUUUH?!

WHERE DID THOSE COME FROM?!
THEY ARE A PRESENT FROM THE EARL.

HE IS AWAY TODAY ...
...
...SO HE DESIRES THAT YOU REST FROM YOUR DUTIES.

THEN TODAY ...

...I DON'T HAVE TO ACCOMPANY EDGAR IN HIS ENDLESS PURSUIT OF AMUSEMENT.

TWO MONTHS HAVE PASSED SINCE I OFFICIALLY BECAME HIS FAIRY DOCTOR ...

...BUT I HAVE YET TO WORK EVEN ONCE!

INSTEAD ...

...HE JUST SHOWS ME OFF LIKE AN ORNAMENT...
...AT THE THEATER, TEAS AND MUSICALES.

DIDN'T HE HIRE ME FOR MY *TALENT*?

A FAIRY DOCTOR HELPS HUMANS AND FAIRIES COEXIST.
BACK IN SCOTLAND, PEOPLE THOUGHT I WAS ODD.
BUT FAIRIES DO EXIST, EVEN IN THE 19TH CENTURY...
...SO I WAS EXCITED ABOUT MY NEW POSITION, BUT...

KA-CHAK
GOING OUT... ...MISS LYDIA?

SINCE I DON'T HAVE TO WORK...
...I THOUGHT I WOULD TAKE A WALK.

I EXPECT THE FOG WILL BE THICK THIS AFTER-NOON.
YOU CAN PREDICT IT?
WHY, YES...

THE HUMIDITY MAKES THE FINS ON MY BACK ITCH.
Heh Heh.
OH, RIGHT.
DON'T WORRY ...
...I WON'T BE LONG!
EVEN THOUGH ...
...IT'S PAST EASTER ...
...SPRING NEVER SEEMS TO COME.

I MISS THE COUNTRYSIDE.
I LIVED IN A SMALL TOWN, BUT I LIKED IT.
IT WAS BURSTING WITH GREENERY.
LOTS OF FAIRIES LIVED THERE.
AND IT WAS FILLED WITH MEMORIES OF MY MOTHER, WHO DIED WHEN I WAS YOUNG.

IF IT WEREN'T FOR MY JOB, I WOULD HAVE GONE BACK BY NOW.

HMPH!

NICO!

YOU'RE COMING, TOO?

THE FISH HERE TASTES AWFUL!

EVEN STRAY CATS WON'T TOUCH IT!

I REFUSE TO EAT IT!
HOP
NICO?
WHAT'S THAT?

IT'S A "CANNED GOOD"!
A HOBGOBLIN NAPPING UNDER THE EAVES SAID IT'S THE BEST FOOD IN LONDON!
I TRADED SOME WALNUT BREAD FOR IT!
OH, TINNED FISH.
FISH ?!
LIKE IT SAYS ON THE LABEL.
PICKLED FISH WITH HERBS.
NO WAY!
WHY'S IT SO HARD?!
THE FISH IS INSIDE.
YOU NEED A SPECIAL TOOL TO OPEN IT.
SO THIS ...
...IS JUST THE CON- TAINER ?!
Tap
AND INSIDE ...
Tap
...IS FISH ?!

ARGH!

THAT HOBGOBLIN TRICKED ME!!

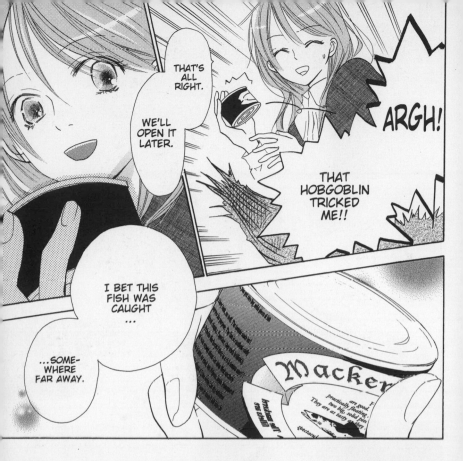

THAT'S ALL RIGHT.

WE'LL OPEN IT LATER.

I BET THIS FISH WAS CAUGHT ...

...SOME-WHERE FAR AWAY.

I LOVE GREEN PLACES LIKE THIS.
THE WEATHER ISN'T GREAT ...
...BUT THAT MEANS NOT MANY PEOPLE ARE OUT.

COME ON, NICO ...
...CHEER UP AND WE'LL—

?

HM?
HE LEFT ALREADY?
WELL, THE FOG IS GATHERING ...

RUSTLE
I SHOULD GO, TOO.

RUSTLE
GRRR
GASP!
A MAN DRESSED IN BLACK ...
THE FOGMAN ?!

STAB
!
THUD
...
R...

RAVEN!
!!
WATCH OUT!
SLASH

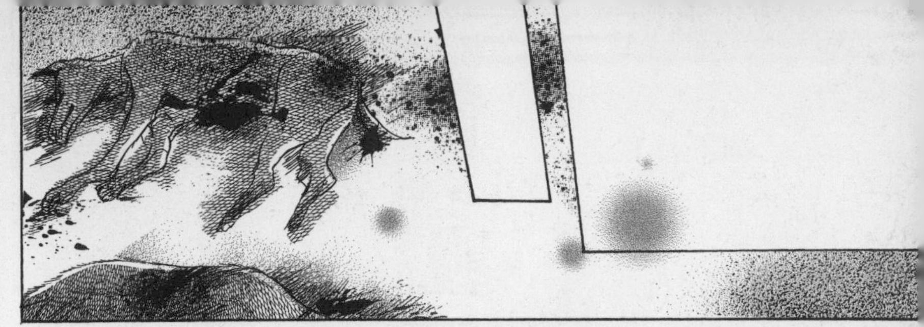

MISS LYDIA ...

...WE SHOULD ...

...LEAVE.

WHAT?

WHAT IS...

...GOING ON?

MISS LYDIA …
…ARE YOU INJURED?
TH-THUMP
NO…
…I'M FINE.
VERY WELL THEN.
Chak
…
HOW CAN HE STAY SO CALM?
TUMP

BUT HE WASN'T A FAIRY.
...WAS THAT MAN?
AND WHO ...
WAS HE A KIDNAPPER?
...AS IF HE WERE THE FOGMAN.
HE APPEARED OUT OF THE FOG ...
WHY WOULD HE WANT ME?
KA-CHAK
LYDIA!
I'M GLAD YOU'RE SAFE.
YES.
IT'S LUCKY ...
...YOU HAD RAVEN FOLLOW ME.
...

I MUST PROTEST!
WOULD I DO SOMETHING SO LOW?
...
I MERELY APPOINTED HIM AS YOUR BODY-GUARD.
ARE YOU ALL RIGHT?
YOU LOOK PALE.
I'M FINE.
A LITTLE BLOOD DOESN'T—
BLOOD?
YOU KILLED THEM?
YES.
HOW MANY WERE THERE?
ONE MAN AND FOUR ANIMALS.
FOUR ANIMALS?
YES.
HE HAD DOGS WITH HIM.
...

TNK
I ALSO ...
...PICKED UP SOMETHING MISS LYDIA DROPPED.
Mackerel Fillets
OH ...
I didn't even notice...
... THANK YOU.
LYDIA ...
...FROM NOW ON, YOU MUST TAKE A MAID OR RAVEN WITH YOU WHEN YOU GO OUT.
YOU MUST NOT GO UNACCOMPANIED.
W-WHY ?!
YOU'RE OVER-REACTING!
I'M NOT AN ARISTOCRAT, SO—
THIS ISN'T SCOTLAND. IT IS HER MAJESTY'S CAPITAL.
YOU MAY NOT CARE, BUT OTHERS WILL JUDGE YOU BY YOUR APPEARANCE AND BEHAVIOR.

YOUR FATHER IS A FAMOUS SCHOLAR ...
...SO IT'S TIME TO ACT LIKE A LADY.
...RATHER THAN A DISTURBING ECCENTRICITY.
...
THINK OF IT LIKE THIS.
IF YOU ACT WITH DECORUM, WHEN YOU TELL PEOPLE YOU CAN TALK WITH FAIRIES ...
...THEY WILL ACCEPT IT AS AN ENDEARING PERSONALITY TRAIT ...
I SEE.
YOU MEAN THE WAY A FORMER **OUTLAW** WEARS AN ARISTOCRATIC MASK.
EXACTLY.
IT MAKES SENSE, BUT ...
NO...
...I WON'T DO THAT.

...
YOU JUST WANT ...
...SOMEONE YOU CAN SHOW OFF AT THE THEATER!
WELL, YOU CAN'T FOOL ME!
I WON'T WASTE MY TIME ANYMORE ON—
NO, LYDIA.
!
I TREAT YOU LIKE A LADY ...
...BECAUSE THIS HOUSEHOLD NEEDS YOU.

WHAT ...?
YOU HELPED ME ATTAIN MY TITLE.
IT DOESN'T BELONG TO ME ALONE.
IT EXISTS BECAUSE OF YOU.
AS A FAIRY DOCTOR ...
...YOU ARE A VALUABLE PARTNER TO ME.
TH-THUMP
WHAT ARE ...
...
...YOU SAYING?
I'M SAYING ...

...THAT I WANT YOU ...

...BY MY SIDE FOREVER.

GASP!

S...
STOP IT!
SHUP
I GET YOUR POINT, SO BACK OFF!!

I CAN'T LET MY GUARD DOWN FOR A SECOND...

NOTHING I SAY PLEASES YOU.
SHALL I TALK ABOUT A FAIRY INSTEAD?
HUH?

THE FOGMAN?!
WHAT ABOUT HIM?!
A WOMAN IS HERE ASKING ABOUT HIM.
COULD THERE BE A CONNECTION...
...WITH WHAT HAPPENED TODAY?
SHE WISHES TO SPEAK WITH YOU.
SHE WANTS...
...YOUR OPINION AS A FAIRY DOCTOR.
CAN YOU MEET HER RIGHT NOW?

...!
ARGH!
HE'S GOT LYDIA IN HIS POCKET!
I HOPE SHE'S ALL RIGHT ...

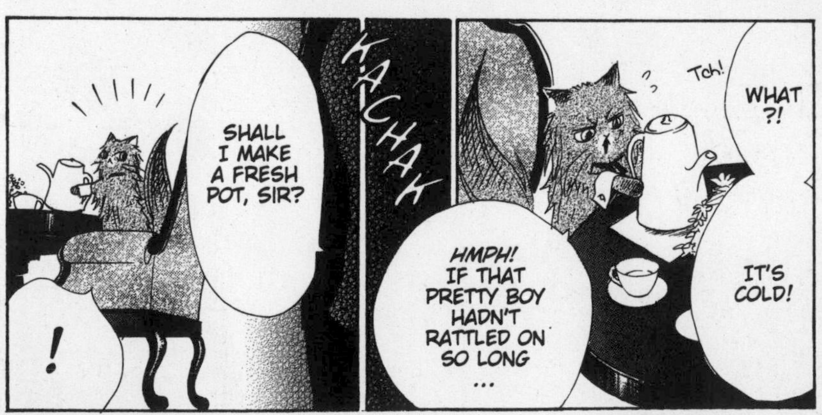

SMILE

YES...

...AND MAKE IT HOT!
HMM...

THIS BUTLER...
...REALLY DOES HAVE MERROW BLOOD IN HIM.

THAT MAKES THINGS EASIER.
HEY, BUTLER...
...WHAT IS THE EARL PLANNING?

HE IMMEDIATELY NOTICED I'M NOT A CAT.

SIGH...

WHATEVER DO YOU MEAN?

THE OTHER DAY, HE WENT OUT ALONE ...

...AND WORE GRUBBY CLOTHES TO BLEND IN WITH THE COMMON FOLK.

HAS HE SAID ANYTHING?

SIGH ...

THE EARL DID THAT?

I FIND IT HARD TO IMAGINE.

AND THAT'S NOT ALL.

WHO WAS THAT GIRL IN HIS CARRIAGE ...

...THREE DAYS AGO?

OH?

WAS SOMEONE WITH HIM?

HE CALLED HER ...

...LADY WALPOLE.

IS HE CHASING HER NOW, TOO?

I AM AFRAID ...

...I COULDN'T SAY.

HMPH

HE'S NO HELP AT ALL.

...

TNK

Mackerel Fille

with herbs

OH!

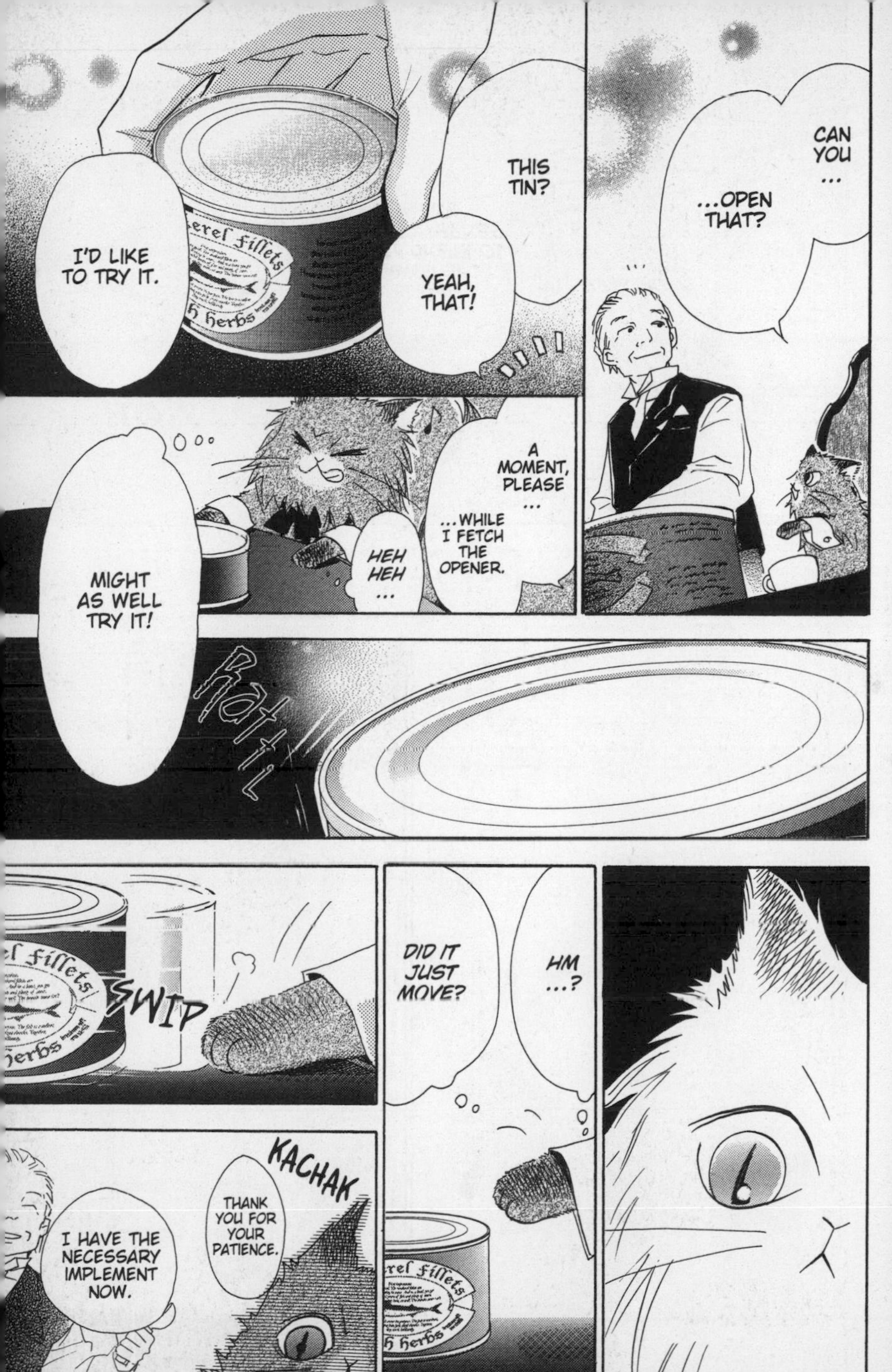
CAN YOU ...
...OPEN THAT?
THIS TIN?
YEAH, THAT!
I'D LIKE TO TRY IT.
A MOMENT, PLEASE ...
...WHILE I FETCH THE OPENER.
HEH HEH ...
MIGHT AS WELL TRY IT!
RATTL
HM ...?
DID IT JUST MOVE?
SWIP
KACHAK
THANK YOU FOR YOUR PATIENCE.
I HAVE THE NECESSARY IMPLEMENT NOW.

I WILL USE THIS ...

...TO CUT IT OPEN.

NO!

WAIT!

WAP

HUH?

IS THERE A PROBLEM?

...

I THINK I'LL ...

...HOLD OFF A BIT.

Mackerel Fillets with herbs

MRS. MARLE.

...!

MY LORD ...
THANK YOU FOR WAITING.
THIS IS LYDIA CARLTON, MY FAIRY DOCTOR.
OH MY!
YOU'RE SO YOUNG!
YOU MAY FIND WHAT I HAVE TO SAY DISTURBING.
I THOUGHT ALL WITCHES WERE OLD, BUT ...
WITCH ...?
IF IT'S ABOUT FAIRIES, I'LL BE FINE.
YOU MENTIONED ...
...THAT YOU SUSPECT THE FOGMAN HAS TAKEN BARONESS DORIS WALPOLE?
YES.
SHE HASN'T RETURNED HOME FOR THREE DAYS.
HER MAID SAYS THEY BECAME SEPARATED AT THE CHARITY BAZAAR ...
...AND SHE HAS BEEN MISSING EVER SINCE.

LADY DORIS IS ONLY 16, BUT SHE HAS ALREADY LOST BOTH PARENTS.

SHE LIVES WITH HER UNCLE AND COUSIN, WHO IS ONE YEAR OLDER.

I USED TO BE THEIR GOVERNESS.

I QUIT WHEN I MARRIED, BUT I AM STILL CLOSE WITH DORIS.

AN INCIDENT LIKE THIS COULD DAMAGE HER PROSPECTS ...

...SO I AM KEEPING MY SEARCH QUIET.

PEOPLE JUST LAUGH WHEN I MENTION THE FOGMAN.
...
THE FOG WAS THICK THAT DAY.
ONE COULD ONLY SEE A FEW STEPS AHEAD.

WHY DO YOU SUSPECT THE FOGMAN?
NO ONE BELIEVES IN HIM ANYMORE.
YES, WELL ...
...I DON'T EXACTLY BELIEVE IT MYSELF.
MY APOLOGIES.
AFTER ALL, I CAME SEEKING YOUR COUNSEL.

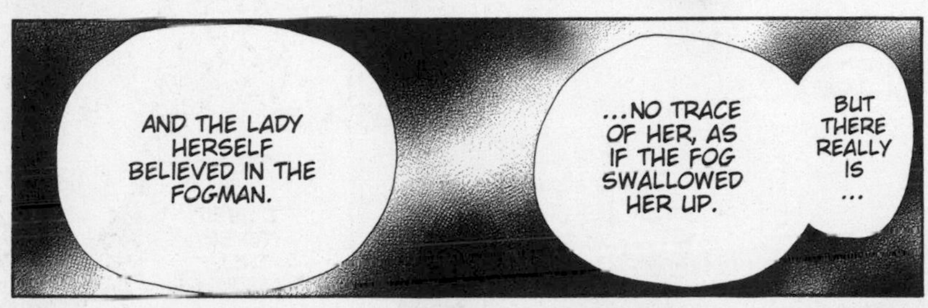
BUT THERE REALLY IS ...
...NO TRACE OF HER, AS IF THE FOG SWALLOWED HER UP.
AND THE LADY HERSELF BELIEVED IN THE FOGMAN.

AS A CHILD, SHE TOLD FORTUNES WITH A FAIRY EGG ...
...AND SAID THAT IF SHE BROKE HER PROMISES TO THE FAIRY ...
...THE FOGMAN WOULD GET HER.
FAIRY EGG?
WHAT ?!
DON'T YOU KNOW WHAT A FAIRY EGG IS?!
URG

THEY'RE POPULAR WITH YOUNG GIRLS.
THEY REST THEIR FINGERS ON A COIN PLACED ON TOP OF THE ALPHABET ...
...AND ADDRESS A FAIRY SAID TO RESIDE IN A GLASS GEM.
FRIENDS MAKE PROMISES TO THE FAIRY ...
...AND ASK IT QUESTIONS.

AND THE FAIRY MOVES THE COIN?
ACTUALLY, ONE OF THE PLAYERS MOVES IT SUB-CONSCIOUSLY.
NONETHE-LESS, GIRLS LOVE IT.

IT SOUNDS LIKE HE'S DONE IT ...
BUT MRS. MARLE ...
...A FAIRY EGG IS A MERE TOY ...
...THAT GIRLS SIMPLY IMAGINE HAS POWER.

MAYBE A FAIRY REALLY DOES MOVE IT.
IF THE GLASS ATTRACTED A FAIRY'S ATTENTION ...

...IT MIGHT COME NEAR AND TELL A FORTUNE.
AND IF YOU OFFEND IT ...
...IT MIGHT TAKE YOU AWAY!

OH ...
BUT ISN'T IT STRANGE ...
...HOW LADY DORIS WAS AFRAID OF THE FOGMAN?
LYDIA ...
...COULD A DIFFERENT FAIRY HAVE TAKEN HER, OUT OF MISCHIEF?
IT'S POSSIBLE, BUT ...
...THE FOGMAN IS LIKE A DEMON, A MASS OF EVIL INTENT.
HE WOULDN'T BE INTERESTED IN A COIN GAME.
I CAN'T SAY YET, BUT—
WELL, WILL YOU TAKE THE JOB?
THIS **IS** YOUR LINE OF WORK, ISN'T IT?

OF COURSE!
I'LL FIGURE OUT WHO'S BEHIND THIS— WHETHER HUMAN OR FAIRY!
I'M HAPPY TO HELP!
...!
...
UM ...
...WILL YOU SUMMON A SPIRIT ...
...OR ASK A CRYSTAL BALL?
WILL YOU DO IT RIGHT NOW?
UH ...
SHE THINKS I'M A MEDIUM OR FORTUNE-TELLER ...
...WELL ...
...I CAN'T SOLVE PROBLEMS WITH MAGIC.
I JUST KNOW A LOT ABOUT FAIRIES.

I CAN ONLY LOOK FOR CLUES A FAIRY MAY HAVE LEFT BEHIND.
...
OH ...
I SEE.
I GUESS IT'S NOT THAT EASY ...
OH NO...
...I DISAPPOINTED HER.
OF COURSE.
SHE CAME HERE SEEKING AN ANSWER...
...AND WAS PREPARED TO REVEAL A DELICATE SITUATION.
MY WORK...
...IS HARD FOR OTHERS TO UNDER-STAND.
...

DON'T GIVE UP HOPE, MRS. MARLE.
HM?
JUST AS YOU ARE QUESTIONING PEOPLE...
...LYDIA WILL ASK FAIRIES.
IF NO PEOPLE WERE AROUND WHEN LADY DORIS DISAPPEARED...
...FAIRIES MAY BE THE ONLY ONES WHO SAW ANYTHING.
EDGAR!
WINK

THANK YOU, MY LORD.
YOU ARE THE ONLY ONE WHO TOOK ME SERIOUSLY.
AND YOU SUGGESTED I TALK WITH MISS CARLTON.
THANK YOU.
I MYSELF KNOW VERY LITTLE ABOUT FAIRIES.
HUH?!
EDGAR SUGGESTED THIS MEETING?!

I THOUGHT HE DIDN'T BELIEVE IN THE FOGMAN!

AND HE SAID FAIRY EGGS ARE JUST TOYS!

I'M GLAD YOU ACCEPTED THIS JOB, LYDIA.

I KNOW ...

...YOU'LL ALWAYS HELP SOMEONE IN NEED.

...?

CHAK

OH...

...YOUR CLIENT LEFT?

IT WAS YOUR FIRST ONE IN A WHILE.

YES.

HOW DID IT GO?

BARONESS DORIS WALPOLE HAS DISAPPEARED.
THE FOGMAN MAY HAVE TAKEN HER ...
...BUT I'M NOT SO SURE.
SHE WENT TO THE CHARITY BAZAAR ...
...THREE DAYS AGO ...
...WHEN THE FOG WAS SO THICK AND—
THREE DAYS AGO?!

THAT'S WHEN ...

...I SAW HER WITH EDGAR IN HIS CARRIAGE!

HUH?!

IS THAT TRUE?!
AH-HA!
HE DIDN'T MENTION THAT?
...
I'M SURE HE'S INVOLVED SOMEHOW!
YOU SHOULDN'T STICK YOUR NOSE INTO IT.
I SMELL TROUBLE!
EDGAR...
...IS UP TO SOMETHING AGAIN!

The Earl & the Fairy

The Earl & the Fairy

London.
The Carlton residence.
...
THREE DAYS AGO?!
THAT'S WHEN I SAW HER WITH EDGAR!
BARONESS WALPOLE HAS BEEN MISSING FOR THREE DAYS ...
NO MATTER HOW YOU LOOK AT IT...

...IT'S SUSPICIOUS.
SURELY...
...EDGAR DIDN'T ABDUCT HER!
WHY WOULD HE DO SUCH A THING?
TO SELL HER!
PRETTY WOMEN FETCH A GOOD PRICE!

BUT...
...HE HAS MONEY AND STATUS.
OH?
BUT HE'S BEEN SLUMMING IN DOCKSIDE TAVERNS.

I CAN SMELL HIS GUILT!
ASKING YOU TO FIND THE BARONESS IS JUST A DIVERSION!
...
IS EDGAR...

...USING ME AGAIN?

HERE.

LOOK AT THIS.

A NEWSPAPER CLIPPING?

"A WHITE-SLAVE RING MAY BE RESPONSIBLE..."

"...FOR CHILDREN DISAPPEARING INTO THE LONDON FOG."

I FOUND IT IN THE EARL'S ROOM.

ENGLISHMEN IN BRAZIL HAVE RESCUED A BOY...

...WHO CLAIMS HE WAS ABDUCTED IN LONDON, LOADED ONTO A SHIP WITH OTHER CHILDREN, AND SOLD TO A FARM.

MEANWHILE, CHILDREN CONTINUE TO DISAPPEAR FROM THE STREETS OF LONDON...

...LENDING CREDIBILITY TO TALES OF ABDUCTION BY THE FOGMAN.

HE HAD OTHER SIMILAR CLIPPINGS.
HE'S DEFINITELY UP TO SOMETHING.
LIKE THE PARK THE OTHER DAY ...
DID EDGAR DO THAT, TOO?!
BUT...
...EDGAR WAS SOLD INTO SLAVERY AS A CHILD.
MAYBE HE'S JUST INVESTI-GATING THAT.
HE HIMSELF WAS A VICTIM ...
DO YOU THINK IT WAS A COINCI-DENCE?
B...
BUT ...
...SO SURELY HE WOULDN'T ...
MISS ...
...YOU'LL BURN THE BISCUITS.
!

OH!

THEY'RE NOT BURNT!

GOOD!

I WONDER IF THEY'LL TASTE LIKE MOTHER'S!

TODAY IS SUNDAY ...

...SO I WANT TO FORGET ABOUT EDGAR AND ENJOY MYSELF.
FATHER WILL BE HOME, TOO.
ONE BY THE WINDOW...
...AND ANOTHER...
...IN THE OVEN.
THAT SHOULD DO IT.
FAIRIES LOVE HERBED SHORT-BREAD.
FATHER!
I BAKED BISCUITS!
WOULD YOU LIKE SOME TEA AND—
HM?

MR. LANGLEY!
OH!
MISS CARLTON!
I HOPE I'M NOT INTRUDING.
YOU'RE JUST IN TIME.
Oh!
IT'S BEEN A WHILE SINCE I BAKED BISCUITS.
HERE, HAVE SOME.
THANK YOU!

PRO-FESSOR CARLTON ...
...THE HOUSE IS MUCH BRIGHTER WITH LYDIA HERE.

WAS IT REALLY SO DARK BEFORE?
IT WASN'T DARK ...
...SO MUCH AS INTIMIDATING FOR WOMEN.
YOU SHOULD AT LEAST PUT AWAY THOSE SKULLS.
FOR LYDIA'S SAKE.

Hmm ...
BUT THEY HELP ME RELAX ...
DO THEY UPSET YOU, LYDIA?
NO, FATHER.
NOT AT ALL.
AH ...
...YOU ARE TRULY YOUR FATHER'S DAUGHTER.
IF ALL WOMEN WERE AS UNDER-STANDING AS YOU ...
...MORE SOLITARY SCHOLARS WOULD SEEK COMFORT IN MARRIAGE.
ARE YOU HERE TO WOO LYDIA, MR. LANGLEY?
I'll try one ...
Ha Ha!
ARE YOU WORRIED, PRO-FESSOR?
IF A MERE COMMENT LIKE THAT UPSETS YOU ...
...WHAT WILL YOU DO WHEN SHE BRINGS HOME A MAN?
Hmph!
LYDIA IS STILL A CHILD!
FATHER...
...

THIS IS FUN.
IT'S BEEN SO LONG SINCE I ENJOYED SUCH QUIET TIME.
NO WONDER IT FEELS GOOD...
I DON'T HAVE TO LOOK AT THAT SCOUNDREL'S FACE!
SIR...
GUH!
NO, NO, NO!
SEND HIM AWAY!
LYDIA!
...EARL IBRAZEL IS HERE...
...TO SEE MISS CARLTON.
WE CANNOT TURN THE EARL AWAY!
SHOW HIM IN.
YES, FATHER.
...

GREETINGS, PROFESSOR CARLTON.

WELCOME TO MY HOME, LORD IBRAZEL.

THANK YOU FOR THE KINDNESS YOU HAVE SHOWN MY DAUGHTER.

IT'S MY PLEASURE.

THIS IS MY ASSISTANT, MR. LANGLEY.
PLEASED TO MEET YOU, LORD ASHENBERT.
HE'S RUINING MY DAY OFF!
COME, LYDIA...
...WHERE ARE YOUR MANNERS?
WELL...
...WHAT DO YOU WANT?
LYDIA!

Sorry...
I THINK FATHER...
...HAS NOTICED THAT EDGAR ISN'T A NORMAL EARL.
PLEASE, HAVE A SEAT, MY LORD.
LYDIA BAKED BISCUITS.
BUT EDGAR IS MY EMPLOYER...
...SO FATHER CAN'T BE RUDE.
AND I GUESS...
...I CAN'T EITHER.
NOW ISN'T THAT INTERESTING...
I MUST TRY ONE.
...

"INTERESTING"?!
PROFESSOR CARLTON...
...I READ YOUR MOST RECENT PAPER.
OH?
ARE YOU A STUDENT OF NATURAL HISTORY?

NATURE IS AN EVER-UNFOLDING MYSTERY.

THE WORD "WONDROUS" CAN BARELY DESCRIBE IT.

YOUR ANALYSIS OF CRYSTALLINE STRUCTURES WAS FASCINATING.

I SAY...

...YOU REALLY **DID** READ IT!

Ha Ha Ha...

FATHER...

...DON'T LET HIM FOOL YOU!

I'M SURE ALL HE DID...

...WAS GLANCE THROUGH IT.

PROFESSOR, THE OTHER DAY...

...I READ ABOUT SOMETHING...

YES.

...CALLED A **FAIRY EGG** IN SOME OLD DOCUMENTS.

THERE IS A STONE BY THAT NAME.

IS IT REALLY A FAIRY'S EGG?
IN MINERALOGY...
...IT'S THE NAME FOR A RARE FORM OF AGATE.
OH, YES.
I HAVE A SPECIMEN HANDY.
YES, HERE IT IS.
TNK
IT LOOKS...
...LIKE THE ROCK HAS ENGULFED THE GEM.
YOU MUST SPLIT IT TO SEE INSIDE.
BUT THIS ISN'T A FAIRY EGG, IS IT?
NO.
THAT IS A KIND OF AGATE, THOUGH.

A FAIRY EGG IS A BEAUTIFUL, MILK-WHITE STONE WITH GREEN STRIATIONS.
THE "PEPPERMINT LEAF" COLORING IS RARE IN ITSELF ...
...
...BUT A FAIRY EGG ALSO CONTAINS WATER SEALED INSIDE IT.
WATER?
DO YOU SEE THE CAVITY IN THE CENTER?
YES.
IN SOME CASES, WATER BECOMES TRAPPED IN THERE.
I THINK THEY'RE CALLED FAIRY EGGS ...
...BECAUSE THE WATER AND THE COLOR OF THE VEINS CAUSE THEM TO RESEMBLE AN EXOTIC CREATURE.

BUT, FATHER ...
...WHAT IF A FAIRY WENT INSIDE ONE?
A FAIRY?
SOMEONE COULD USE THAT MYSTERIOUS WATER ...
...TO LURE AND CAPTURE A FAIRY!
THERE ARE RECORDS ...
...OF USING A FAIRY EGG ...

...TO SEAL A DEMON.
DO FAIRY EGGS STILL EXIST?

I SUPPOSE SO.
THERE WAS ONE IN THE 16TH CENTURY, AT A MONASTERY IN CANTER-BURY.
THERE ARE NO MENTIONS OF THEM IN LATER RECORDS, HOWEVER.
HMM ...

...?

BUT, EDGAR ...
...FAIRY EGG FORTUNE-TELLING JUST USES GLASS GEMS.
IS THERE SOME CONNECTION?
NO, NOT AT ALL.
I'M SIMPLY INTERESTED.

I KNOW WHERE THEY SELL ...
...THE FAIRY EGGS USED IN FORTUNE-TELLING.
WOULD YOU LIKE TO GO SEE?
HUH?
NOW ?!

I CAME HERE TO INVITE YOU.
THERE'S AN EVENT AT CREMORNE GARDENS ON SUNDAYS.
PRO-FESSOR CARLTON ...
...MAY YOUR DAUGHTER ACCOMPANY ME?
IN AN OFFICIAL CAPACITY, OF COURSE.
WELL ...
...I HATE TO INTER-FERE, BUT ...

IT'S ALREADY EVENING...
...AND THE PLEASURE GARDENS HAVE A BAD REPUTATION.
I WILL SEE YOU HOME AFTER-WARDS.
BESIDES, I WILL BE WITH YOU. DON'T WORRY.
SHALL WE, MISS CARLTON?
YES...
...ALL RIGHT.
THERE GOES MY DAY OFF...
...BUT I SHOULD SEE THESE FAIRY EGGS.
BESIDES...
...I NEED TO ASK EDGAR SOMETHING.
JUST A MOMENT.
I NEED TO GET READY.
OH, UH...
...MISS CARLTON?
YES?

THESE ARE FOR YOU.
I ALWAYS SHOW UP EMPTY-HANDED, SO ...
OH MY!
ANYWAY, I, UM ...
...I EN-JOYED YOUR BISCUITS, SO ...
THANK YOU, MR. LANGLEY!

TUNK

PLEASE, WATCH YOUR STEP.

...

...
RATTL
KREAK
WHAT IS IT?
WHY ARE YOU STARING AT ME?

I DON'T THINK I'VE EVER ...
...SEEN YOU SMILE LIKE THAT.

HM?

YOU LOOKED TRULY PLEASED WHEN MR. LANGLEY GAVE YOU THOSE FLOWERS.
BUT NOT WHEN I DID.
BUT ...
...THAT WAS JUST—

I UNDER-STAND.
GIRLS WOULD RATHER HAVE WILD-FLOWERS PICKED IN A DITCH FROM THE MAN THEY ADORE ...
...THAN A GORGEOUS HOTHOUSE BOUQUET FROM A MAN THEY COULD CARE LESS ABOUT.

LEAVE IT BE. I WANT TO ASK YOU SOME-THING.

THE DAY LADY DORIS DISAPPEARED ...

...SHE WAS IN YOUR CARRIAGE.

YOU WENT TO THE DOCKS THAT DAY.
LADY DORIS HAS BEEN MISSING EVER SINCE.
WHAT WERE YOU DOING AT THE DOCKLAND WARE-HOUSES?
THAT IS EXTREMELY SUS-PICIOUS!

HMM ...
WHO TOLD YOU THAT?

ARE YOU CLAIRVOYANT?

LITTLE FAIRIES RODE BACK IN YOUR CARRIAGE ...
...AND MENTIONED WHAT THEY HAD SEEN.
OR SO NICO SAID ...

... I SEE.

IF WE GET MARRIED, I WON'T BE ABLE TO STRAY.
IF YOU CAN'T BE FAITHFUL, DON'T GET MARRIED!

I DID INVITE LADY DORIS INTO MY CARRIAGE, BUT I TOOK HER HOME.
WE MERELY MET BY CHANCE.
HER DIS-APPEARANCE SURPRISED ME MORE THAN ANYONE.

...SO WHY IS IT...

YOU'RE NOT HIDING ANYTHING?

NO.

...I WOULD RATHER BELIEVE HIM...

...THAN DOUBT HIM?

WELL ...

...HERE WE ARE, LYDIA.

OH!

SO THIS IS ...

...CREMORNE GARDENS!

OH MY!

...

IT'S SO BIG... AND SO MANY PEOPLE...

LYDIA?

Oh!

OOPS. I'M NOT ...

...HERE TO HAVE FUN.

S...

SORRY!

WHERE SHALL WE GO?

I RECOMMEND THE ELEPHANT SHOWS.

HUH?

FINE.

BUT AFTERWARD, WILL YOU SPEND TIME WITH ME?

I...

...WANT TO BE WITH YOU BECAUSE THIS IS YOUR DAY OFF.

...!

WHAT?!

THERE YOU GO ...
...TEASING ME AGAIN!
LYDIA ...
...IS MY DESIRE TO SPEND TIME WITH YOU ...
...REALLY SO UN-BELIEVABLE?
YOU MUSTN'T BE SO NEGATIVE.
YOU'RE QUITE ATTRACTIVE.
I WANT TO KNOW YOU BETTER. AND I WANT YOU TO KNOW ME.
THAT IS WHY I INVITED YOU.
...
ALL RIGHT.
WE CAN ENJOY OUR-SELVES A LITTLE.

SO WE DON'T BECOME SEPARATED.

HE'S...

...MANIPULATING ME...

...AGAIN.

THIS BUILDING ...

...ADVERTISES A FAIRY SHOW.

OOOOH!

THIS ...

...IS A FAIRY SHOW?

FWIP

FWIP

Clap Clap

THE IDEA IS THAT INVISIBLE FAIRIES BEAR THE CARDS ALOFT.

IT'S JUST SLEIGHT OF HAND.

THERE AREN'T ANY FAIRIES.

I knew it.

THEY'RE SELLING THE FAIRY EGGS OVER THERE.

I'LL GO BUY ONE. WAIT HERE.

SO? IS ANYTHING INSIDE?
HMM...
IT'S JUST GLASS. I DON'T SEE ANYTHING TO ATTRACT A FAIRY.
SEE?
THE COLOR IS MUDDY—NOT PRETTY AT ALL.
AND IT'S JUST HOLLOW INSIDE.
BUT IF THERE WAS SOMETHING INSIDE THAT FAIRIES LIKE...
SO IT'S UNLIKELY FAIRIES ARE BEHIND LADY DORIS'S DISAPPEARANCE.
YES, BUT...
...IT'S TOO SOON TO BE SURE.
HOLD ONTO IT FOR NOW.
KRACK

Murmur
DID SOMEONE DROP A FAIRY GLASS?
Murmur
KRACK
EEEK!
?!
Eek!
Agh!
KRACK
Murmur
What happened ?!
MISS, YOU MUST BE CAREFUL ...
...HOW YOU TREAT FAIRIES.
Murmur
YOU CANNOT BE ROUGH OR SAY ANYTHING RUDE ...
...OR THEY WILL GROW ANGRY AND BREAK THEIR EGGS.
Murmur
HE'S GOT TO BE KIDDING ...
Murmur
WHAT ...?
Murmur

PERHAPS THERE'S A GAS INSIDE THAT EXPANDS WITH HEAT.
OR MAYBE THOSE PEOPLE WERE PLANTS...
EITHER WAY, IT'S A DANGEROUS TRICK.
...
HEE HEE...
HEE HEE...
UP THERE!
HEE HEE...
?!

A BOGEY-BEAST?!
...
OH ...
...YOU CAN SEE ME?
GASP!
EDGAR!
LET GO OF THE GLASS!
HM?
KRACK

...
LYDIA ...
...WHAT JUST HAPPENED?
FOR NOW ...
...LET'S JUST GET OUT OF HERE.
THERE WAS ...
...A BOGEY-BEAST BACK THERE.
BOGEY ...?
A FAIRY?
A MEAN ONE.
THEY AREN'T SMART, BUT THEY'RE MEMBERS OF THE UNSEELIE COURT OF EVIL FAIRIES.
DID HE BREAK THE FAIRY EGGS?
THE SHOWMAN WASN'T SURPRISED, SO THERE MAY HAVE BEEN PLANTS ...
...BUT I'M CERTAIN THE BOGEY-BEAST JOINED IN.

DID HE JUST HAPPEN TO BE THERE...

...OR IS HE SOMEHOW...

...RELATED TO THE FAIRY EGGS?

ARE YOU HURT?

N...

NO.

...

OH ...

...I'M GLAD.

WELL, NOW THAT OUR ERRAND IS DONE ...

...SHALL WE TAKE A BOAT OUT ON THE LAKE?

HUH ?!

WAIT JUST A MOMENT!

YOU CALL THAT **DONE** ?!

YOU CANNOT REFUSE ME.

YOU **PROMISED.**

BUT ...

...WE'VE GOT IMPORTANT THINGS TO DO!

YOU ALMOST INJURED THE EARL!
I TOLD YOU TO HURT THE GIRL!
A BOGEY-BEAST?!
...
BUT, MISTRESS...
...SHE CAN SEE ME!
AND THAT'S NOT ALL!
SHE KNOWS I BROKE THE GLASS!
SHE'S A FAIRY DOCTOR!
SO?!
YOU'RE MY SERVANT!
DO AS I SAY!

...
YES ...
...MISTRESS.
DO SOMETHING DREADFUL ...
...TO SCARE HER OFF!
I WANT HER TO DISAPPEAR FROM LONDON—JUST LIKE DORIS!

The Earl & the Fairy

I WONDERED WHO WAS VISITING THE EARL...
...BUT IT TURNS OUT...
...SHE'S NO ONE TO WORRY ABOUT.
HER HAIR IS A DIRTY RUST COLOR.
BUT I HAVE TO ADMIT...
...HER GOLD-GREEN EYES STAND OUT.
BUT STILL...
Hmph.
...I'M A MUCH BETTER MATCH FOR THE EARL!

TCH!
THAT FAIRY DOCTOR CAN SEE ME.
BAH!
THAT BRAT DOESN'T KNOW...
...I ONLY OBEY HER BECAUSE MY MASTER ORDERED ME TO.
IF SHE INTERFERES WITH THE PLAN...
...ALL MY MASTER'S WORK WILL BE FOR NAUGHT!

AS USUAL, THE EARL IS PLOTTING SOMETHING...

...SO WE'D BETTER BE CAREFUL.

...

WHAT A BEAUTIFUL PLACE.
THE EARL AND I LIVE IN DIFFERENT WORLDS.
LYDIA ...

HOW DO YOU LIKE OUR SPECIAL SEATS?
SEATS?
A DAY AT CREMORNE GARDENS MUST END WITH FIRE-WORKS.
THEY LOOK BEST FROM THE LAKE.
WE'RE GOING TO WATCH FIRE-WORKS?
YES.
HAVE YOU SEEN THEM BEFORE?
NO.
WELL THEN...
...I COUNT MYSELF FORTU-NATE...
...TO BE PRESENT FOR YOUR FIRST EXPERIENCE.
Glug
Glug

A TOAST...
...TO MY DEAR FEARLESS FAIRY DOCTOR.
Ching
FEAR-LESS?
WHY DO YOU SAY THAT?

YOU HELPED ME EARLIER...

...WITHOUT FEAR OF INJURY.

...

FINE, BUT "MY DEAR" WAS UNNECESSARY...

...EDGAR'S EMBARRASSING WORDS AND DRAMATIC FLAIR...

...HAVE BECOME A PART OF MY LIFE.

SOMEHOW...

AND AS I GAZE AT THIS GOLDEN CHAMPAGNE...
...EVERYTHING ELSE SEEMS SO SMALL.
EDGAR?
WHERE HAVE YOU SEEN FIREWORKS BEFORE?

FIREWORKS?
YES.
TODAY ISN'T YOUR FIRST TIME, IS IT?

I WONDERED WHERE YOU MIGHT HAVE...
...SEEN THEM.
OOPS...
I SAW THEM...
...WHEN I WAS A CHILD.

THE MANOR HOUSE HOSTED PARTIES WITH FIREWORKS.
THERE WAS A LAKE ON THE GROUNDS...
...AND BOATS UPON THE WATER.
...
GOOD...
IT WASN'T A BAD MEMORY.
EDGAR WAS RAISED AS AN ARISTOCRAT BUT SOLD INTO SLAVERY.
I DON'T WANT TO REMIND HIM OF THAT.
AND I DON'T WANT TO GET ANY MORE INVOLVED.

I DECIDED...
...NEVER TO ASK HIM ABOUT HIS PAST.
HUH ?!
...
DON'T YOU WANT TO HEAR MORE?
WH- WHY WOULD I?!
I'M NOT INTERESTED IN YOUR PAST!!
OH NO...
...I SOUNDED SO HARSH AGAIN.
WHAT I MEAN IS ...
...UM ...
...THE FUTURE IS MORE IMPORTANT THAN THE PAST.
YOU'RE OFFICIALLY AN EARL NOW...
...SO THE PAST DOESN'T MATTER.
UGH...
WHAT A SUPERFICIAL THING TO SAY.

THEN ALLOW ME ...
...TO TELL YOU ABOUT AN ACQUAINTANCE OF MINE.
HE HAD ...
...ONE OF THE AGATE FAIRY EGGS.
THAT'S ...
WHILE TALKING WITH YOUR FATHER TODAY ...
...I REALIZED IT WAS ONE WITH A DEMON INSIDE.
BUT HE LOST IT WHEN HE WAS A CHILD.
HOW DID HE LOSE IT?

HE DOESN'T REMEMBER CLEARLY ...
...BUT HE THINKS THE FOGMAN ABDUCTED HIM.
WHAT ...?
HE AWOKE IN A DARK PLACE ...
...UNABLE TO MOVE, AS IF BOUND BY MAGIC ...
...AND UNABLE TO FLEE.
THEN TWO FAIRIES ...
...APPEARED TO HIM IN THE FORM OF GIRLS.

HALF-UNCONSCIOUS, HE ASKED THEM FOR HELP.

THEY RESPONDED...

..."WHAT WILL YOU GIVE US IN EXCHANGE?"

ALL HE HAD WAS THE FAIRY EGG...

...SO HE GAVE IT TO THEM.

THEY SAID...

..."WE WILL HELP YOU," THEN DISAPPEARED.

DID THEY EVER HELP HIM?

NO.
I THINK HE WAS IN A WAREHOUSE SOMEWHERE.
AFTER-WARD, HE WAS PUT ON A BOAT TO AMERICA AND SOLD.

THE SAME THING HAPPENED TO EDGAR. IS THAT HOW THEY MET?
IS HE STILL IN AMERICA?
NO, HE DIED.
AND YOU ...
...WANT TO FIND THE FAIRY EGG FOR HIM?
NO, LYDIA.
I WANT TO FIND HIM.
THE FOGMAN ...
...MAY STILL HAVE HIM IMPRISONED.
SOMETIMES I THINK HE IS STILL IN DARKNESS.
I HOPE HE IS ...

...BECAUSE THEN I CAN HELP HIM.
AFTER ALL, I HAVE AN EXCELLENT FAIRY DOCTOR.

LYDIA ...

...WILL YOU HELP HIM?

IT HAS NOTHING TO DO...

...WITH HIS OWN PAST...

...BUT ...

...EDGAR WANTS TO HELP HIS FRIEND.

HIS COMPASSION SURPRISES ME.

THANK YOU.

I...

...WILL DO ANYTHING I CAN.

WH...
WHAT ARE YOU—
I'VE ALWAYS THOUGHT ...

...YOU SMELL LIKE CHAMOMILE.
LIKE THOSE BISCUITS YOU BAKED.
TH-THUMP
WH...
TH-THUMP
WHAT IS HE...
FWOOO
POOOM
?!
OHH ...

POOM
OH MY!
THEY'RE AMAZING!
SO PRETTY!
POOM
POOM
OH!
ANOTHER ONE!
HA...
...THE FIRE-WORKS!
Ha
Ha
Ha
Ha
WH...
WHY ARE YOU LAUGH-ING?!
THEY REALLY ARE AMAZING!

MY HOPES CRUMBLE...
...FOR THE FIREWORKS HAVE STOLEN YOUR HEART FROM ME!
WELL...
...OF COURSE! I MEAN—
OOH, LOOK!
THERE'S THE EARL!
WHAT A COINCIDENCE!
WHY IF IT ISN'T...
...LADY ROSALIE WALPOLE.
HOW HAVE YOU BEEN?
OH, SIMPLY PEACHY!
IMAGINE BUMPING INTO YOU HERE!
...
WALPOLE?

OH, THAT'S RIGHT ...
...LADY DORIS LIVED WITH HER COUSIN AND UNCLE.
GOOD EVENING, LORD IBRAZEL.
I AM ROSALIE'S UNCLE—GRAHAM PURCELL.
I HAVE SEEN YOU AT THE CLUB IN PICCADILLY ...
...BUT THIS IS OUR FIRST TIME MEETING PROPERLY.
I KNOW OF YOU, SIR.
THEY SAY YOU ARE QUITE THE PLAY-BOY.
...
HMM?
MY LORD ...
...WHO IS THAT WITH YOU?
THEY'RE RIVALS IN DEBAUCHERY ?!
FORGIVE ME ...
Gack

...YOU HAVE NOT MET.
THIS IS MISS LYDIA CARLTON.
STARE
HMM.
TO WHICH CARLTONS DO YOU BELONG?
WHAT DOES YOUR FATHER DO?
...
I'M A FAIRY DOCTOR.

OH, THE SPECIALIST EVERYONE IS TALKING ABOUT?
WE LOOK ABOUT THE SAME AGE.
TOO BAD YOU HAVE TO WORK FOR A LIVING.
...
WORK?
AS MY CONSULTANT, LYDIA IS MORE LIKE MY PARTNER.

BY THE WAY...
...WHERE IS LADY DORIS? YOU TWO ARE PRACTICALLY INSEPARABLE.
SHE IS IN THE COUNTRY...
...RECOVERING FROM ILLNESS.
I AM SORRY TO HEAR THAT.
YOU MUST MISS HER.
OH, NOT SO MUCH.
SHE'S TOO TIMID AND ALWAYS CLINGS TO ME.
NOW I DON'T HAVE TO BABYSIT HER ANYMORE.
...
SUCH HARSH WORDS...
...ABOUT HER MISSING COUSIN.
OR IS SHE HIDING SOMETHING?
MY LORD...

...MAY I JOIN YOU?
IF MISS CARLTON ISN'T ENOUGH TO SATISFY YOU, THAT IS! ♪
ROSALIE ...
...THAT'S RUDE.
EDGAR...
IT IS ALL RIGHT, PURCELL.
I DON'T MIND.
REALLY?!
...MUST LIKE HER.

OH, JOY!
I ASKED MY UNCLE TO BRING ME ...
...BUT HE'S OLD AND BORING!
THEN MAY I...
LEAVE MY NIECE WITH YOU, MY LORD?
I ADMIT I DO HAVE BUSINESS TO ATTEND TO.

YES.

IT IS AN HONOR TO BE IN THE COMPANY OF SUCH A BEAUTIFUL LADY.

YOU EMBARRASS ME...

Glance

...LORD IBRAZEL! ♡

...

SHE CAME AT THE RIGHT TIME.

I NEED TO LEAVE.

FATHER WILL WORRY IF I'M OUT LATE.

...

I SEE.

OH?

WHY?

THEN IT CAN'T BE HELPED.

RAVEN.

ESCORT LYDIA HOME.

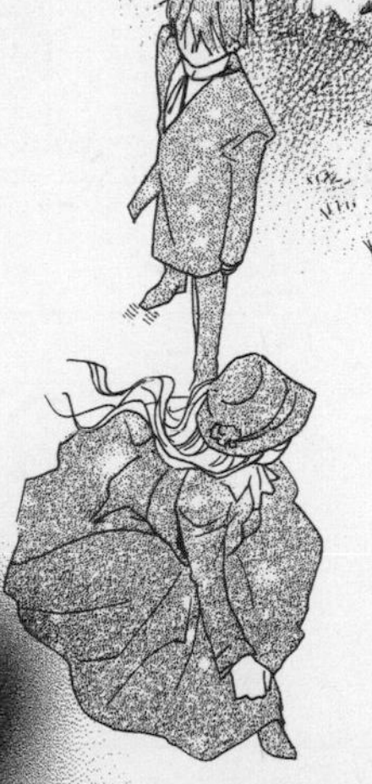

AND I DON'T CARE!

GIRLS...

...WOULD RATHER HAVE WILD-FLOWERS PICKED IN A DITCH FROM THE MAN THEY ADORE...
...THAN A GORGEOUS HOTHOUSE BOUQUET FROM A MAN THEY COULD CARE LESS ABOUT.

SLAM

...
WHY DID HE SAY THAT?!
HE'S SO WOMAN-CRAZY!
I BET HE SAYS THAT TO ALL THE GIRLS!
I'M GLAD I CAME BACK.
THIS WAY FATHER WON'T WORRY.
...
ANYWAY, I ONLY WENT TO DO MY JOB!
LYDIA!
!!
GASP!

NICO ...
...YOU FOLLOWED US?
YEAH.
MY HUNCH WAS RIGHT.
HE WENT INTO BARONESS WALPOLE'S TOWNHOUSE.
SOME GIRL WITH CURLY ORANGE HAIR WAS ORDERING HIM TO CAUSE TROUBLE!
!

WELL ...

...HE SAID HIS TRUE MASTER IS SOMEONE ELSE.

HIS MASTER ORDERED HIM TO OBEY HER.

WHO IS HIS TRUE MASTER?

I DON'T KNOW.

I DON'T THINK SHE KNOWS.

...

THEN SHE'S IN DANGER.

FAIRY DOCTORS HAVE ALWAYS HELPED ...
...THOSE WHOM BAD FAIRIES TRICK.

IF WHAT NICO SAYS IS TRUE...
...THE BOGEY-BEAST MAY BE TRAPPING HER.

BEFORE SHE'LL TELL ME ABOUT LADY DORIS...
...I NEED TO SEPARATE HER FROM THAT BOGEY-BEAST.
BUT...
...I DOUBT ROSALIE WILL LISTEN TO ME.
HOW CAN I CONVINCE HER OF THE DANGER?
UGH...
SHE'S SO SNOOTY.
THIS IS MORE COMPLICATED THAN I EXPECTED.
EVEN THOUGH THE GLASS GEMS FOR FORTUNE-TELLING...
...AND THE AGATES KNOWN AS FAIRY EGGS ARE DIFFERENT...
...EDGAR LINKS THEM TOGETHER...
...JUST LIKE LADY DORIS LINKED FORTUNE-TELLING...
...WITH THE FOGMAN.

...FOR A MOMENT...

...I FELT LIKE I WAS ONTO SOMETHING.

THE WALPOLES ARE NEWLY RISEN ...

...AND NOUVEAU RICHE.

LADY DORIS IS A BARONESS IN HER OWN RIGHT, AND ONLY SIXTEEN.

HER PARENTS DIED AT SEA TEN YEARS AGO.

I SUSPECT ROSALIE AND GRAHAM ARE PUSHING DORIS ASIDE SO THEY CAN CONTROL THE FAMILY FORTUNE.

DORIS HAS HIGH RANK, BUT ROSALIE ACTS SUPERIOR AND SHAMES HER IN FRONT OF OTHERS.

DORIS IS A REAL WEAKLING.

I SAID IF SHE BROKE OUR PROMISE TO THE FAIRY EGG, THE FOGMAN WOULD GET HER.
SHE WAS ACTUALLY SCARED!
SHE FLED LONDON TO HIDE IN THE COUNTRY.
WHAT A COWARD!
ROSALIE WAS VERY FORTH-COMING.
I HAD MET HER BEFORE, IN GROUPS OF OTHERS...
IT WAS DISAPPOINTINGLY EASY.
...BUT SHE RESPONDED TO MY EVERY QUESTION.
WELL...

...WHAT ...

...IS MY NEXT MOVE ...

...IN LEARNING ABOUT THE BARONESS?

LORD EDGAR ...

...WELCOME BACK.

THANK YOU, RAVEN.
HOW IS LYDIA?
WAS SHE JEALOUS?

JEAL-OUS?
IF SHE GREW JEALOUS AFTER SEEING ME ...
...WITH ANOTHER WOMAN, THEN I HAVE A CHANCE, RIGHT?

MY APOLO-GIES, LORD EDGAR.
I DID NOT KNOW I WAS TO CONFIRM HER EMOTIONAL STATE.
...
OF COURSE.
I UNDER-STAND.

RAVEN ...
...NEVER CHANGES.
AND YOUR ASSIGNED TASK?
YES.
I AM HAPPY TO REPORT ...
...THAT MISS LYDIA RETURNED HOME SAFELY.
DID YOU SEE ANY-ONE SUS-PICIOUS?
NO.
NO ONE AT ALL.
CHAK
...
FUMP
I SEE.
PERHAPS I WORRY TOO MUCH.
I WAS CERTAIN HE WOULD SEE LYDIA RETURNING HOME ...
...AS THE PERFECT CHANCE.
OH WELL.
HE'D NEVER DO ANYTHING HIMSELF, ANYWAY.
PERHAPS EVEN HIS MINIONS WERE UN-PREPARED.

IF I MAY ...
...MY LORD ...
CHAK
YES?
ARE YOU CERTAIN IT'S ALL RIGHT TO USE MISS LYDIA THIS WAY?

EVEN IF IT ISN'T HIM ...
... IT'S BEST TO DRAW HIM OUT AND REMOVE THE DANGER, FOR LYDIA'S SAKE.
HE...
...PUT ME ON A SHIP TO AMERICA AND TURNED ME OVER TO PRINCE.
THIS IS STRIKINGLY SIMILAR.
BUT IS HE A COMMON CRIMINAL OR ONE OF PRINCE'S MINIONS?

BUT ...
...WOULD HE TARGET MISS LYDIA?
THE MAN IN THE PARK MAY HAVE BEEN A MERE COINCIDENCE.
YES, HE WOULD.
HE KNOWS THAT PRINCE PAYS A FORTUNE FOR INDIVIDUALS WITH SPECIAL ABILITIES.
IN RECENT YEARS, PSYCHICS HAVE BEEN DIS-APPEARING FROM LONDON.

HE WOULDN'T MISS THE CHANCE FOR A FAIRY DOCTOR.
HE'LL MAKE ANOTHER MOVE.
...
YES.

I WILL HAVE MY REVENGE ...
...AND SHOW PRINCE THAT I AM STILL ALIVE ...
...AND FIGHTING BACK.

JUST A LITTLE LONGER.

SOON I WILL AVENGE EVERYONE.

MY LORD...

...

...DO YOU DO THIS FOR ERMINE AND THE OTHERS?

IF SO, I DO NOT THINK THEY WOULD WISH IT.

THAT MAY BE SO...

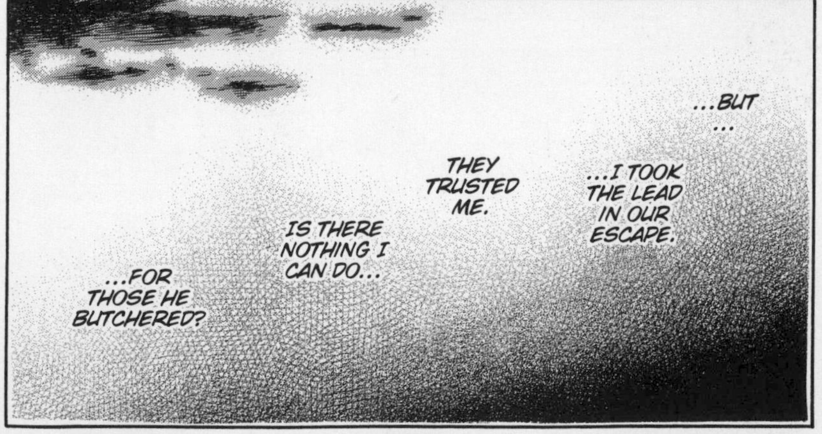

CAN I GO ON LIVING HAPPILY...
...WHILE THEY REMAIN UNAVENGED?

CAN I THROW AWAY THE PAST...

...AND FORGET IT ALL...

...EVEN THOUGH THEIR SACRIFICE...

...MADE MY OWN ESCAPE POSSIBLE?

NO, I COULD NEVER...
...DO THAT.
RAVEN...

...YOU ARE...
...THE ONLY ONE LEFT.

NO ONE ELSE...

...MADE IT THIS FAR.

BUT I PROMISED TO SET THEM FREE.

I KNOW...

...THAT VICTORY...

...WILL NOT BRING BACK THOSE I LOST.

...A GAME OF SORTS.

WHY ARE YOU APOLOGIZING?
NO ONE ...
...REGRETS WHAT HAPPENED.
WHEN I LOOK AT YOU NOW ...
...I BELIEVE YOU ARE HAPPY IN YOUR HEART ...
...BUT ...
...
...I CANNOT FIND THE RIGHT WORDS.
THIS MAY BE...
...A FOOLISH GAME...
...BUT ONCE I HAVE BEGUN ...
THAT'S ENOUGH ...
...RAVEN.
...I *MUST* WIN.

The Earl & the Fairy

ROSALIE ...
...IS CONTROLLING THE BOGEY-BEAST.
THERE MAY BE A CONNECTION WITH LADY DORIS'S DISAPPEARANCE.
FAIRIES CAN BE DANGEROUS IF YOU'RE NOT CAREFUL.
WILL YOU WARN HER ABOUT IT?
...
NO?
I THINK SHE WOULD LISTEN TO YOU.
YOU'RE GOING TO SEE HER AGAIN, AREN'T YOU?
IN OTHER WORDS ...
...YOU AREN'T JEALOUS AT ALL.
HUH ...?

The Earl & the Fairy

WHY WOULD I BE JEALOUS?

HMPH

YOU CAN DALLY WITH WHOMEVER YOU WANT.

THIS WAY, I DON'T HAVE TO WASTE MY TIME WITH YOU.

THAT'S RIGHT.

I WOULDN'T BE JEALOUS...

...OVER THIS PLAYBOY!

NOW BACK ON TOPIC...

...ROSALIE SHOULD WEAR A CROSS OF ROWAN TO KEEP THE BOGEY-BEAST AWAY.

IF THAT DOESN'T WORK, I'LL THINK OF SOME-THING ELSE.

sigh...

YOU'RE MORE UN-APPROACH-ABLE THAN EVER TODAY...

NOK

NOK

?

MASTER...

...YOU HAVE A VISITOR.

UGH...

TMP

SPEAK OF THE DEVIL!
EDGAR!
OH, HOW I'VE MISSED YOU!
EVER SINCE WAKING UP, I'VE BARELY BEEN ABLE TO STAND IT!
SHE SAW HIM *YESTERDAY*...
GOOD MORNING, ROSALIE.
YOU LOOK EVEN MORE STUNNING TODAY.
EDGAR...
...THE WATTS ARE HOSTING A MUSICALE WITH A VIENNESE PIANIST.
WOULD YOU LIKE TO GO?
OF COURSE!
MRS. WATTS ONLY INVITED CLOSE ACQUAINTANCES.
WILL I BE WELCOME?
EVERYONE WANTS TO KNOW ABOUT YOU!
...
Ignored.

I SHOULD LEAVE...
ROSALIE...
...YOU SHOULD WEAR A CROSS OF ROWAN.
MY FAIRY DOCTOR...
...SAYS IT WILL KEEP AWAY EVIL FAIRIES.
HUH?
!

EDGAR...
...IF YOU MENTION ME, SHE'LL REJECT IT!
MISS FAIRY DOCTOR...
...SPARE ME YOUR WILD ACCUSATIONS.
IT ISN'T AN ACCUSATION.

YOU KNOW THERE'S A BOGEY-BEAST HANGING AROUND YOU.
HE'S A DANGEROUS FAIRY.
THAT'S NOT TRUE!
HE PROTECTS ME!
HOW WOULD YOU KNOW ANYWAY?!

HE'S JUST PRETENDING!
IF HE'S AROUND, SOME-THING BAD WILL HAPPEN!
HE MAY HAVE CAUSED LADY DORIS'S ILLNESS!
...

ARE YOU SAYING THAT'S MY FAULT?
THAT I DID IT?!

NO, BUT—
IT'S NOT MY FAULT!

WE SWORE ON THE FAIRY EGG, BUT SHE BROKE HER PROMISE!
SHE'S A COWARD, AND SHE OFFENDED THE FAIRY ...
...SO SHE HAD TO GO CALM HER NERVES IN THE COUNTRY!
IT'S HER OWN FAULT!

I'M TOTALLY BLAME-LESS!
...
HMM ...

ROSALIE SAID SHE WISHED DORIS WOULD DISAPPEAR...

...BUT SHE ACTS LIKE SHE TRULY BELIEVES DORIS IS SICK.

THE BOGEY-BEAST COULD STILL BE INVOLVED, THOUGH.

ROSALIE...

...THE BOGEY-BEAST MAY BE TRYING TO TRAP YOU...

...SO...

GIVE IT UP.

I'M ON TO YOUR SCHEMING!

WHAT?!

Scheming?

YOU DON'T LIKE HOW CLOSE I AM TO EDGAR!

THAT'S WHY YOU'RE INSULTING ME!

BUT REALLY, YOU MUST STOP.

YOU'RE SIMPLY NO MATCH FOR MY GOOD LOOKS!

HUH?!

HUUUH ?!
SO STAY OUT OF MY WAY!
WHAT'S WRONG WITH YOUR EYES, ANYWAY?
!
THEY'RE LIKE A WITCH'S.
THEY MAKE PEOPLE UNCOM-FORTABLE.
WHAT ...?
MAYBE FAIRY DOCTORS AREN'T EVEN HUMAN.
ARE YOU A FAIRY IN DISGUISE?
SNAP
YOU'RE NO PICTURE YOURSELF, YOU KNOW!
HOW MANY HOURS DID YOU SPEND IRONING THE KINKS OUT OF THAT ORANGE MESS?!
Amusing...
HUH ?!
WELL AT LEAST MY HAIR ISN'T LIKE FILTHY RUST!
RUST ?!

MY HAIR IS THE COLOR ...
...OF CARAMEL!
Hmf!
LET'S SETTLE THIS RIGHT NOW!

...
Tee Hee
I STILL HAVEN'T TASTED THE CARAMEL.
DOES THAT MEAN...
...!
KACHAK
THIS IS RIDICULOUS!
I'M LEAVING!
Tee Hee
WHAT A NAIVE GIRL!
SLAM

I CAN'T BELIEVE HIM!
HE'S SO FAST WITH WOMEN!
"TASTED" ?!
Rattle
SHUF
!
...
WHAT AM I DOING?
REALLY ...
...IT HAS NOTHING TO DO WITH ME.

I DON'T CARE WHO THAT SHALLOW PLAYBOY ...
...KISSES ...
...
GACK
YES?!
WHAT IS IT ?!
KNOCK BEFORE ENTERING!
MY APOLOGIES.
YOU DID NOT RESPOND.
OH ...

WAS I SO ANGRY THAT I DIDN'T HEAR ANYTHING?
SORRY.
BUT ...
... SHOULDN'T YOU BE WITH EDGAR?

MISS LYDIA ...
...LORD EDGAR IS NOT AS SHALLOW AS YOU THINK.

HE HEARD ME...
HE DOES HAVE A GLIB TONGUE ...

...BUT HE NEVER FORCES HIMSELF ON ANYONE.

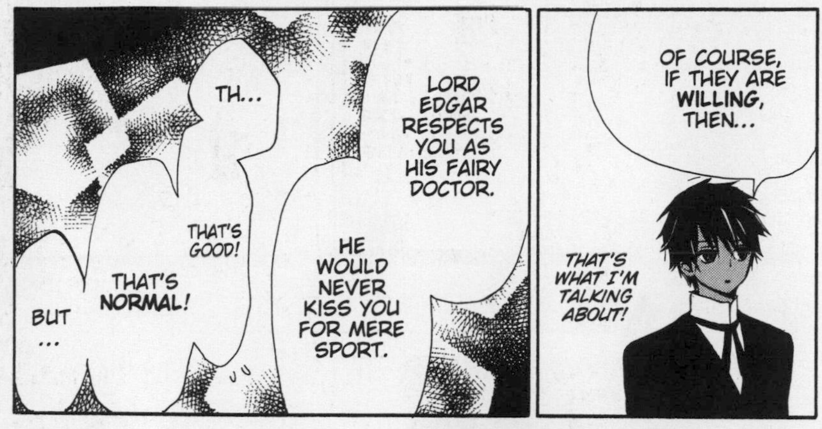
OF COURSE, IF THEY ARE WILLING, THEN...
THAT'S WHAT I'M TALKING ABOUT!
LORD EDGAR RESPECTS YOU AS HIS FAIRY DOCTOR.
HE WOULD NEVER KISS YOU FOR MERE SPORT.
TH...
THAT'S GOOD!
THAT'S NORMAL!
BUT ...

...HOW CAN I BELIEVE THAT?
IF I HAD LET MY GUARD DOWN ...
...WHO KNOWS WHAT WOULD HAVE HAPPENED YESTERDAY!
DO NOT WORRY.
HE WOULD NOT DO ANY-THING.
I AM SURE OF IT.
...
RAVEN IS ALWAYS SO LOYAL.

SHALL WE WAGER ON IT?
...!
HE'S SO CONFI-DENT...
ALL RIGHT ...
IT'S A BET!

AND ONE MORE THING ...

TNK

I FOUND THIS.

...

IT'S...

...A STRIPED AGATE!!

Gasp!

WH ...

WHERE DID YOU FIND THIS?!

IN THE DRAWING ROOM.

PATTERNS LIKE PALE GREEN VEINS ...

...

Slosh

...WITH WATER INSIDE...

THIS IS WHAT ...

...FATHER WAS TALKING ABOUT!

THAT ...

...MUST MEAN ...

...THIS IS ...
...A FAIRY EGG!

A REAL ONE?
WHAT'S IT DOING HERE?
Well then...
MISS LYDIA ...
...IF YOU WILL EXCUSE ME ...

IS A DEMON SEALED INSIDE?
IS THIS THE ONE EDGAR'S ACQUAINTANCE HAD?
IF IT WAS IN THE DRAWING ROOM...
...DOES THAT MEAN ROSALIE DROPPED IT?

RAVEN ...

TELL ME ...
...DO YOU REMEMBER WHAT EDGAR SAID ...
...ABOUT A BOY KIDNAPPED FROM LONDON ...
...WHO LATER DIED IN AMERICA?
YES.
IS THAT TRUE?
IF HE WAS EDGAR'S FRIEND, YOU WOULD KNOW HIM.

MANY OF OUR FRIENDS MET THAT FATE.

LORD EDGAR DID NOT MEAN ONE SINGLE PERSON.

IN ANY CASE ...

...THEY ARE ALL DEAD NOW.

PRINCE KILLED THEM.

HE DOES NOT FORGIVE TRAITORS.

CHILDREN DISAPPEARED INTO THE FOG...

...AND WERE SOLD INTO SLAVERY.

EDGAR MUST HAVE MEANT THAT HE WANTS ...
...TO RESCUE THEM ALL.

HE WANTS TO SAVE THE SOULS OF ALL THOSE CHILDREN...
...AS WELL AS HIS OWN.
HOW-EVER ...

...HE WAS TALKING ABOUT WHAT HAPPENED TO HIM-SELF ...
...WHEN HE MENTIONED THE TWO FAIRIES WHO APPEARED.
I HAVE HEARD THAT STORY BEFORE.
IS IT ALL RIGHT TO TELL ME THAT?
WELL, HE HAS NOT TOLD ME NOT TO.
HOWEVER, I DO NOT KNOW ABOUT THE FAIRY EGG.
OH ...
I SOMEHOW SUSPECTED AS MUCH...
...BUT, DOES THAT MEAN...
...EDGAR GAVE THE FAIRY EGG TO THOSE FAIRIES?
MISS LYDIA ...
...I WOULD GLADLY GIVE MY LIFE FOR LORD EDGAR.
THE OTHERS FELT THE SAME WAY.
HOW-EVER ...

...IT IS HARD FOR LORD EDGAR ...
...EVEN IF THOSE WHO PASSED AWAY HARBOR NO REGRET.
YES ...
...I IMAGINE SO.
HE WAS OUR MASTER AND LEADER.
WITHOUT EVER COMPLAINING OR ASKING FOR HELP ...
...HE ALONE BORE THE WEIGHT OF EVERY-ONE'S TRUST.
EVEN NOW ...
...HE IS FIGHTING THE PAST ALONE.
...
MISS LYDIA ...
...PLEASE DO NOT HATE LORD EDGAR.

HUH ...?
HE IS NOT PERFECT, BUT DO NOT ...
...LOSE HOPE IN HIM.
PERFECT? HIM?
HE'S SHALLOW, AND A VILLAIN, AND A LIAR!
HE'S FULL OF CHARACTER FLAWS!
...
YES, AND THAT IS ALL RIGHT.
WHAT ...?
WHAT DOES THAT MEAN?
RAVEN WANTS ME TO ACCEPT EDGAR THE WAY HE IS?
?
BUT WHY IS IT SO IMPORTANT THAT I DO SO?
OH, RIGHT ...
I'M SORRY, RAVEN ...
...BUT MAY I LEAVE EARLY TODAY?
EDGAR ISN'T HERE ANYWAY.
DO YOU FEEL UNWELL?
NO.
THERE'S SOMETHING I WANT TO DO.

CREAK

LYDIA'S GONE ...

GOOD.

FWUF

...SO THIS IS MY CHANCE!

SWIP

ROSE-MARY ...

...SAGE ...BASIL ...

LOTS OF AROMATIC HERBS ...

AH!

HERE IT IS!

A REST AMONG CASKS ...
...AND ATOP ROSEMARY ...
CAN SUCH A WONDROUS PLACE TRULY BE?
AH, THE DECEIT ...
A CANNERY?
DOZING IN HERBS ...
...WE AWOKE IN A PRISON ...
...
WHAT ARE YOU?
!
Twitch
YOU GOT TINNED WHILE NAPPING?
I KNEW IT. SOMETHING'S TRAPPED IN HERE.
...IS IT JUST A DUMB FAIRY?
OR...
WHO ARE YOU?
WHO TRICKED YOU?
...
IF YOU TELL ME, I'LL LET YOU OUT.
TCH!
IT DOESN'T TRUST ME.
MAYBE IT THINKS I WANT TO EAT IT ...
...
LYDIA COULD DEAL WITH IT...

...BUT IT MAY NOT BE A GOOD FAIRY.

MAYBE IT'S LOCKED IN THERE BECAUSE IT'S EVIL.

KACHAK

!

UH-OH!

SWIP

KREAK

UGH!

...

IT WOULD BE HIM!
MEOWWW
WELL... YOU KNOW.
I LIKE IT HERE.
I RING A BELL AND THE BUTLER BRINGS TEA!
YOU LOOK SATIS-FIED.
I KNEW IT.
HE CAN UNDER-STAND WHAT I SAY.
I HEARD THAT LYDIA LEFT.
Act nonchalant
DIDN'T YOU GO WITH HER?
WELL THEN ...
CHAK
...LET ME CONFIDE IN YOU MY WORRIES.
WORRIES?
IT'S ABOUT LYDIA ...
HOW CAN I GET HER TO OPEN UP TO ME?
HUNH?!

HER HEART ISN'T SET ON ANYONE, IS IT?
THIS IS MY CHANCE.
SIGH...
HISSS
YOU!
YOU'VE BEEN FLIRTING WITH MISS GINGER CURLS!
YOU'RE JUST TOYING WITH LYDIA!
THAT'S WHY SHE KEEPS HER DIS-TANCE!
YOU LIVE IN DIFFERENT WORLDS ANYWAY!
DON'T YOU DARE STIR HER UP!
SOME-HOW...
...I GET THE FEELING HE JUST SCOLDED ME.
Hmph!
MY APOLO-GIES.
I'LL HAVE THE BUTLER BRING A TREAT.
"TREAT"...?
...!
TNK
LIQUEUR-FILLED CHOCO-LATES.
THEY JUST ARRIVED FROM FRANCE.

DON'T ...

...LIE TO LYDIA.

I UNDERSTAND.

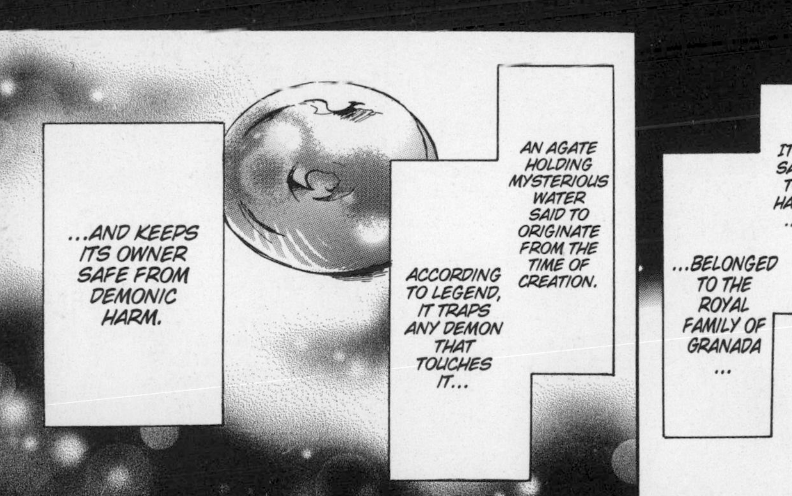

IT IS UNCLEAR HOW IT CAME TO ENGLAND.

BECAUSE OF ITS DELICATE VEIN PATTERN, LIKE THAT OF A LEAF ...

...AND BECAUSE IT IS COM-PARABLE IN SIZE TO AN EGG...

...IT IS CALLED A ***FAIRY EGG***.

FOR YEARS, IT REMAINED IN A MONASTERY.

IT IMPRISONED A DEMON THAT ONCE TERRORIZED LONDON ...

...AND HAS BEEN LOST SINCE THE 16TH CENTURY.

THERE'S NO DOUBT ABOUT IT.

THIS IS IT.

ITS LOCATION IS UNKNOWN.

IT IS SAID TO BE HELD BY A ROYAL FAMILY ...

...OR IN THE HANDS OF AN ARISTOCRATIC COLLECTOR.

FUMP

SO IT WOULDN'T BE STRANGE ...

...IF IT WERE IN EDGAR'S HOUSE.

AND THAT FITS WITH EDGAR MEETING TWO FAIRIES.

BUT ...

...I DOUBT THEY WERE REALLY FAIRIES.

REAL FAIRIES WOULDN'T BREAK THEIR PROMISE.

THEY WERE PROBABLY JUST GIRLS IN PRETTY DRESSES.

IF THEY KEPT THE AGATE...

...THEN ONE OF THOSE GIRLS...

...WAS ROSALIE!

...

HEY!

!

THE BOGEY-BEAST!

WE MEET AGAIN!

NOW GIVE THAT BACK!

!

Chak

UM...

...ALL RIGHT.

Tunk

GO GET IT.

IT'S ON THE DESK.

HA HA!

IF HE KNOWS IT'S DANGEROUS TO HIM...

...THEN WHY IS HE HANGING AROUND ROSALIE?

HERE. I BROUGHT IT.

HEY, CAREFUL!

NOT SO CLOSE!

NO USE TRYING TO TRAP ME!

YOU GO GET IT!

TCH!

HE KNOWS IT WOULD SUCK HIM IN.

WHOOPS...

GAAAAH!
SHUFF
BLAST YOU ...
...GIRL!
IF HE SAW YOU, HE WOULDN'T WASTE A MOMENT—
WHO ARE YOU TALKING ABOUT?
OH, UH ...
...NO ONE!
FORGET ABOUT IT!
JUST GO OUTSIDE!
MISTRESS IS WAITING IN HER CARRIAGE!
SHE CAME TO RECLAIM HER BELONGING!
OH ...?
ROSALIE'S HERE?

...
ROSALIE ...
GET IN.
TUNK
...
THE EARL'S ARABIAN SERVANT ...
...GAVE SOMETHING TO YOU.
YES, I HAVE IT.
BUT, ROSALIE ...
...DO YOU KNOW WHAT IT IS?

IT'S A MAGIC STONE ...
...FOR MAKING MY WISHES COME TRUE.
KLATTER KLATTER
!
WHERE ARE WE GOING?
SOMEWHERE WE CAN TALK.
WE DO NEED TO TALK, DON'T WE?

THE BOGEY-BEAST ...
...ISN'T HERE.
FIRST ...
...HAND OVER THE STONE.
...
UM ...

...HOW LONG HAS THAT FAIRY BEEN WITH YOU?
SINCE YOU FOUND THAT STONE?
NO.
HE SHOWED UP A FEW YEARS LATER.
IT'S A FAIRY EGG.
IT TOOK A WHILE TO HATCH, BUT WHEN IT DID ...
...HE CAME OUT TO SERVE HIS OWNER.
HE TOLD ME SO HIM-SELF.

I KNEW IT.

THE BOGEY-BEAST IS LYING TO HER.

...

WHATEVER IS IN THE AGATE CAN'T COME OUT ON ITS OWN.

WHY DID SOMEONE GIVE YOU...

...SOMETHING SO PRECIOUS?

THAT'S WHY THE BOGEY NEEDS ROSALIE.

UM, MISS WALPOLE?

HOW DID YOU GET IT?

HUH?

...

WHAT ARE YOU TRYING TO SAY?

HE STOLE IT?
REALLY ?
ABSO-LUTELY!
THAT'S WHY THE FAIRY CHOSE ME!

WE'LL BE ABLE TO TALK THERE.
KLIK

...
WE'VE ALMOST ARRIVED ...
...AT THE PLACE WHERE I RECEIVED IT.

KREEAK

TAK
TAK
TAK
IT WAS ...
...EIGHT YEARS AGO ...

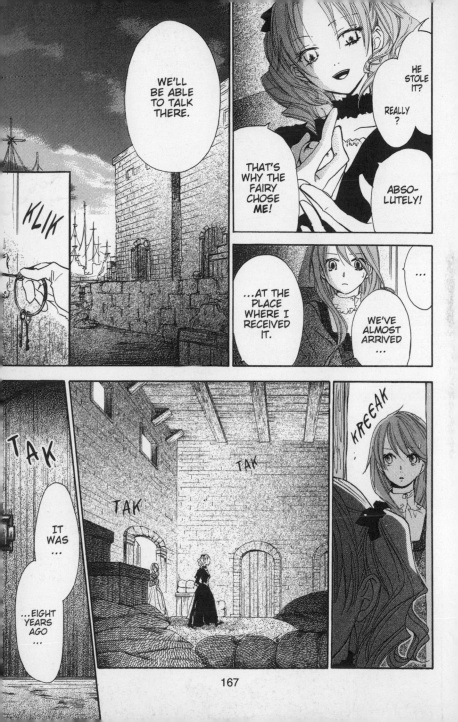

KLAK
A BOY WAS LYING IN HERE.
TAK
HIS CLOTHES WERE BURNT AND HE WAS FILTHY.
TAK
THAT'S HOW I KNEW...
...HE MUST HAVE DONE SOMETHING WRONG.
BUT...
...THAT MIGHT NOT BE TRUE.
OF COURSE IT'S TRUE!

OTHERWISE, HE WOULDN'T HAVE BEEN LOCKED IN HERE!
EVERY GUTTERSNIPE STEALS AT SOME POINT!
...
SHE THINKS LIKE A RICH GIRL...

THAT SHAMELESS BRAT...
...BEGGED US TO HELP HIM.
I OFFERED TO HELP HIM...
...IN EXCHANGE FOR A STONE HE HAD.

IT TURNED OUT TO BE A BEAUTIFUL GEM THAT HE MUST HAVE STOLEN.

I TOLD HIM THAT WE WOULDN'T ...

...HELP A THIEF.

DIDN'T HE GET ANGRY?

I DON'T KNOW.

HE WAS BARELY CONSCIOUS.

DORIS WAS WORRIED HE WOULD COME FOR REVENGE.

HE'S THE REASON DORIS IS AFRAID OF THE FOGMAN.

HE WAS MUMBLING ABOUT THE FOGMAN ...

...SO SHE BELIEVES THE FOGMAN ABDUCTED HIM.

TWO GIRLS WHO LOOKED LIKE FAIRIES...

...ABANDONED HIM...

...

...HERE ON THIS COLD FLOOR.

I DON'T THINK EDGAR...
...REALLY THOUGHT THEY WERE FAIRIES.
THE AGATE WAS THE ONLY PROOF OF HIS BIRTH.
GIVING IT AWAY WAS HIS ONLY HOPE.
BUT THEY DIDN'T HELP HIM.
HE ESCAPED ON HIS OWN AFTER MANY YEARS...
...AND MANY SACRIFICES.
IF HE FINDS OUT THAT ROSALIE AND DORIS...
...WERE THE ONES WHO TOOK THE AGATE...

OR...
...DOES HE ALREADY KNOW?!
...
IS THAT WHY HE'S LOOKING FOR LADY DORIS...
...AND ASKED ME ABOUT THE FOGMAN AND FAIRY EGGS?
UH-OH ...
WHAT IS EDGAR AFTER?
MAYBE INSTEAD OF HELP-ING LADY DORIS, HE WANTS TO ...
!
HUH ?!
SLAM

KLICK
!!
ROSALIE?!
WHAT ARE YOU DOING?!
OPEN THE DOOR!
STOP PLAYING AROUND!
BAM
BAM
I'M NOT PLAYING AROUND.
BAM
OPEN THE DOOR!
BAM
YOU'RE IN MY WAY.
YOU'RE NOT RIGHT FOR THE EARL, SO STAY AWAY FROM HIM.

STAY IN THERE FOR A WHILE.
MY FAIRY SAID THIS WOULD GET YOUR ATTENTION.
TEE HEE!
THE BOGEY-BEAST!
YOU MUSTN'T TRUST HIM!
EDGAR IS PLOTTING SOMETHING, TOO!
DON'T LET HIS SWEET TALK FOOL YOU!
STILL JEALOUS, HUH?
WELL, YOU'LL COOL DOWN IN THERE.
TAKE CARE ...
...LYDIA.

The Earl & the Fairy

Bonus Manga

RAVEN SAW IT!

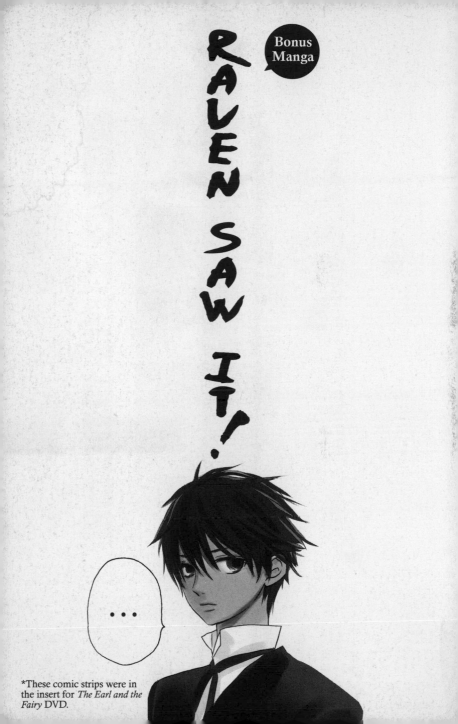

*These comic strips were in the insert for *The Earl and the Fairy* DVD.

1 NICO AND RAVEN

2 JOKE

Have you heard this story?
I know!
I'd like to see you smile just once.

Every day, a stingy man passed by an eel shop, sniffing and saying, "That smells good!"
Then on New Year's Eve, he got a bill from the shop that said "Smelling Fee: 600 mon."
...

Ugh...
He isn't laughing at all...
In fact, he seems a little angry...
Miss Lydia...

...please avoid ruining the British atmosphere of The Earl and the Fairy with Japanese anachronisms.
Oops...

3 XX OUT OF CONTROL

When I draw Rosalie I actually get excited.
It's so cute how selfish she is.

-Ayuko

Ayuko debuted with the story "Us, You and Me" in *Bessatsu Margaret* magazine and has gone on to publish several manga titles in addition to *The Earl and the Fairy*. Born in Kumamoto Prefecture, she's a Leo and loves drawing girl characters.

Mizue Tani is the author of several fantasy novel series and in 1997 received an honorable mention in the Shueisha Roman Taisho awards. Aside from *The Earl and the Fairy*, her other major series is *Majo no Kekkon* (The Witch's Marriage).

The Earl and the Fairy

Volume 3

Shojo Beat Edition

Story and Art by
Ayuko

Original Concept by
Mizue Tani

English Translation & Adaptation/John Werry
Touch-up Art & Lettering/Joanna Estep
Design/Izumi Evers
Editor/Pancha Diaz

HAKUSHAKU TO YOSEI-COMIC EDITION-

First published in Japan in 2008 by SHUEISHA Inc., Tokyo.
English language translation rights arranged with SHUEISHA Inc., Tokyo.

Printed in the U.S.A.

Published by VIZ Media, LLC
P.O. Box 77010
San Francisco, CA 94107

10 9 8 7 6 5 4 3 2 1
First printing, September 2012

www.viz.com www.shojobeat.com

PARENTAL ADVISORY
THE EARL AND THE FAIRY is rated T for Teen and is recommended for ages 13 and up. This volume contains fantasy violence.
ratings.viz.com

Is this girl a devil in disguise... or a misunderstood angel?

A Devil and Her Love Song

Story and Art by Miyoshi Tomori

Meet Maria Kawai—she's gorgeous and whip-smart, a girl who seems to have it all. But when she unleashes her sharp tongue, it's no wonder some consider her to be the very devil! Maria's difficult ways even get her kicked out of an elite school, but this particular fall may actually turn out to be her saving grace...

Only $9.99 US / $12.99 CAN each!

Vol. 1 ISBN: 978-1-4215-4164-8
Vol. 2 ISBN: 978-1-4215-4165-5
Vol. 3 ISBN: 978-1-4215-4166-2
Vol. 4 ISBN: 978-1-4215-4167-9

Check your local manga retailer for availability!

VIZ MEDIA
www.viz.com

This is the last page.

In keeping with the original Japanese comic format, this book reads from right to left—so action, sound effects, and word balloons are completely reversed. This preserves the orientation of the original artwork—plus, it's fun! Check out the diagram shown here to get the hang of things, and then turn to the other side of the book to get started!

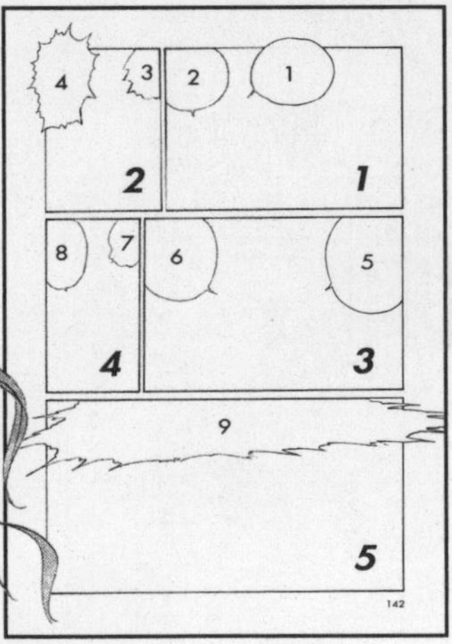